HOW TO START A CRAFT BUSINESS

30 STEPS TO START YOUR BUSINESS THE RIGHT WAY.

By
SARA MILLIS

Copyright © 2017
WWW.MYINDIELIFEBLOG.NET

How to Start a Craft Business

DEDICATION

This book is dedicated to my mother and my partner who have been there every moment of this rollercoaster of an entrepreneurial ride. Thank you for being patient, honest, supportive and for reading every word I write at least 100 times!

More than that, this book is dedicated to all you dreamers and crafters out there who aspire to own their own craft business. I'm here to tell you;

YOU CAN DO IT!

Self-Published
Copyright © October 2017 Sara Millis
WWW.MYINDIELIFEBLOG.NET

All rights reserved.
ISBN-13: 978-1977969538
ISBN-10: 1977969534

How to Start a Craft Business

INTRODUCTION

Starting your own craft business is an extremely exciting time, if not a little scary. There is so much to think about, that sometimes we just don't know where to start!

I've written this book to help get you started in the *right* way, so that you can enjoy everything a thriving craft business has to offer; creativity, joy and of course profit.

It's going to take some work and some courage, but I promise you it will be worth it.

We have a Facebook group where you can join with other creatives on their journey. It's a great place to network and chat, but also a safe place to ask questions. You can find us at www.facebook.com/groups/myindielifeblog/

Sara x

How to Start a Craft Business

Table of Contents

Dedication 2
Introduction 3
Starting Your Journey 8
1. Research 13
   Customer Research 13
   Competitor Research 15
   Market Research 16
2. Narrow Your Focus 17
3. Find Your Customer 20
4. Design Something People Actually Want 23
5. Product Costings 25
   How To Cost Your Idea 27
6. Create a Business Plan 31
7. Choose Your Name 33
8. Design Your Brand 35
9. Consider How To Sell 37
   Online Retail 37
   Shows 38
   Wholesale 39
10. Legalities 40
    HMRC Registration 40
    Trading Standards & Licensing 41

How to Start a Craft Business

Insurance 42
11. Range Plan 43
   Why is a Range Plan so Important? 43
   The Pyramid Range Plan 45
      Top Level Products 46
      Mid-Level Products 46
      Low Level Products 47
      Does This Work For Reproducible Items Only? 47
12. Production 49
   Creating A Production Sample 50
   Creating A Production Plan 52
13. Plan Your Marketing 54
   Your Marketing Message 54
   What is a Marketing Funnel? 55
   A Simple Day 1 Marketing Plan 57
   Being Clear On What You Need To Say 58
14. Set Up Your Website (Or Sales Platform) 59
   What Every Website Needs 60
15. Beautiful Photos 62
   The Difference Between Web Images and Product Listing Photographs 63
      The Web Product Image 63
      The Product Listing Photograph 65
16. Mailing List 68

How to Start a Craft Business

17.	Plan Your Social Media	71
	What Is A Marketing Campaign?	71
	Can I Automate My Social Media?	73
	Don't Forget Engagement	73
18.	Friendly & Professional Customer Service	74
	Presentation	75
	Reputation	76
	Dealing With Problems	76
19.	Accounts & Budgets	79
	Spreadsheets Are Your Friend	79
	Budgeting	80
	Review Your Accounts Regularly	80
20.	Schedule Your Time	81
21.	Support Systems	82
	Streamlining Systems	82
	Sound Board Support	83
22.	Set Goals	84
23.	Keep Motivated	87
	How To Spot Your Lack Of Motivation	87
	Explore What Makes You Feel Unmotivated	88
	Why You Feel Unmotivated	88
	10 Things To Do To Feel More Motivated	89
24.	Set Up Your Workspace	93
25.	Work On It Every Day	95

26. Confidence Is Practice 97
27. Keep Researching 100
28. Remember To Be The Boss 103
    The Employee Mind-Set 104
    The Boss Mind-Set 105
    Why Planning Works 106
29. Keep Reviewing 108
30. Never Be Afraid to Evolve 109
Conclusion 111
About The Author 112
Other Books By Sara Millis 113
Free Video Workshops By My Indie Life Blog 114

STARTING YOUR JOURNEY

I'm going to be brutally honest here and tell you straight that this journey will be a tough one. You will have days when you feel like you are on a high and the next day you will hit rock bottom. This will be especially true at the start when you have no income, no customers and plenty of expenses.

I'll be even more honest and tell you right now that this rollercoaster doesn't change with time. You will still have peaks and troughs.

That is the life of an entrepreneur!

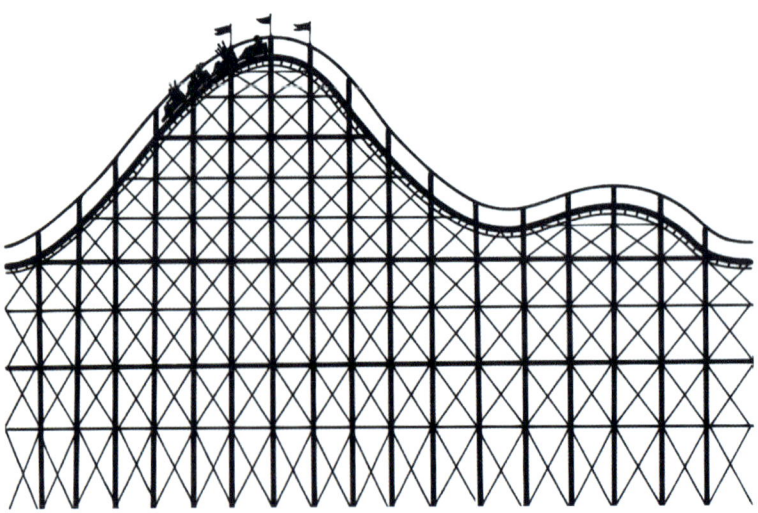

How to Start a Craft Business

There is a wonderful flip side to that though, a reward if you like. Running your own business can be one of the most amazing things you can do for yourself. It's a wonderful space where you can earn money for the life you want, on your terms.

My own journey started in mid-2006, while I was working as a freelance Fashion Designer in London. As was the custom with freelance work in the fashion industry I was tied into a lucrative contract that would only have me work for two days each week.

At this point I must interject with a confession… I'm a workaholic! Or is it that I just have a strong work ethic? I can't decide which, but it does mean I can't sit still if I'm bored.

So with time on my hands and nothing else to do, I decided to try selling on eBay. eBay back in those days was just starting to get really big here in the UK and it was literally impossible not to make a return on a small investment if you worked out a few basic principles. So with one hundred pounds at my fingertips I carefully chose my first stock items.

I stuck to my guns and invested in something I knew about; haberdashery and craft supplies. I found a really great deal on some bankrupt stock, which was from a strong supply line (due to the early signs of recession on the high street).

How to Start a Craft Business

My idea was to create a space where those who had lost shops in their locale could find an on-line replacement.

In a week or so my investment was returned and I had enough to buy two more stock boxes and so I continued my experiment.

Pretty soon my experiment took on some serious pace and I had begun to find focus in wool textiles, something I knew little about, but could see a bigger market for. I started investing in wool products and my journey shifted.

By 2007/8 I found myself buying a fellow eBayer's successful wool business and this is where I started getting serious traction. So much so that I was actually able to give up the day job and make a go of this business full time, relocating to Devon which had been a dream for us.

At no point in this journey had I decided to sit down and plan my business, or see how it was looking financially and this costly mistake was something that would soon come to haunt me.

I think it was about 2010, when I suffered a major burnout that coincided with an unfortunate miscarriage, leaving me almost bed ridden for a month. At this point I did what most people would do; I cried a lot and I started to question everything around me. What am I doing? Why are we living here? Why am I working so hard when life is so short? I questioned everything.

I turned to my business and realised that my experiment had gotten away from me. Whilst I was turning some pretty staggering figures, the truth was I couldn't afford to take on an extra pair of hands to cover the ever growing workload. It was obvious that I hadn't been paying attention to the most basic of business requirements, profitability.

I took pen and paper in my hands and started planning. Planning like I should have done from day one!

I made a lot of changes when I got back to work and I lost customers because of it, but I ended up with a business that I adored and that paid me a real wage for the time I worked on it.

What did I change?

I became a handmade led business creating and selling my own hand dyed yarns and fibres. I also taught and wrote books on aspects of the crafts my customers worked in. I became a 'go-to-person' for my product.

When I closed and sold Sara's Texture Crafts in May 2017 I had turned over almost one million pounds in revenue. That is quite staggering for a craft business trading from my spare room!

How to Start a Craft Business

I realised that I only achieved this through careful planning and working in a focused direction. This is the lesson I want to teach.

It is obvious to me that others struggle to make the same leap from creative idea to successful small business and so I started my second business [My Indie Life Blog](#).

My dream is to help creative folk, like you, make your dream businesses happen.

So let's spend some time together and let me talk you through everything I think you should be doing at the start of your own craft business journey.

1. RESEARCH

I cannot stress to you highly enough, that if you do one thing today for your new business it is that you start your ongoing research process.

Research is not just something that you complete at the beginning, but it is the real backbone to any future decision you make, so it is really important that you continue researching as part of your weekly and monthly business efforts.

There are three types of research you need to be on top of and these answer the following three questions;
- Who is my customer?
- Who are my competitors?
- Where does my product fit into the market?

CUSTOMER RESEARCH

If you know your customer, then you know what to sell and how to sell it to them – fact.

Researching your customer is hard to keep on top of though, because whilst their foundation remains the same, their needs constantly evolve. So getting to know your customer as a person, or social group is incredibly important.

How to Start a Craft Business

The way I used to deal with this when I worked in fashion was to create a customer board. A customer board is essentially a pin board of images and keywords, or phrases that tell you at a glance who your customer is. In fashion terms it would tell me their age, gender, style, their social group and their disposable income. This would allow me to then create a collection of clothes that this 'person' or group of people would want to buy into, because it would be something they felt was socially acceptable to wear, even 'fashionable' and affordable on their terms.

We can take a similar approach with any businesses' customer research. For example, if you were a bank and you wanted to sell a product aimed at first time buyers, then you have to make that product right for that client group, taking into account everything that means something to them when making a decision about banking products. By understanding what it is that they want and how they want it, you can create the perfect product in their eyes.

Once you have a foundation idea of who your customer is, then you need to monitor their behaviour to see how you can adapt your product to fit their evolving needs as a client. In banking terms this might be to adapt your terms, or incentives to suit the economic climate for your client. In fashion terms it might be to throw in this season's pink, over last season's chocolate.

Whilst one of these things might seem more trivial than the other, to your customer who is buying into your specific product at that moment in time, these changes no matter how trivial or fundamental, are incredibly intrinsic to their decision to buy your product over a competitors.

COMPETITOR RESEARCH

Of the three types of research, this is the most common one that I see clients concentrating on and whilst it has its own merits for retrieving invaluable information about the market place, it isn't the whole story. It also isn't a tool by where you can fixate on measuring your success, which is another common mistake people make.

Competitor research is the gathering of information about the products and services that are most similar, or the same as yours. These are the products and services your customers might choose over yours.

Establishing who your competitors are and what they do should help you understand if your pricing and offer is right, or complete. It also helps you to spot how else your customers are buying similar or the same products.

Remember here that competitor research is not about fixating on their perceived success over yours. Your success is in how your customers perceive your products and services!

MARKET RESEARCH

Occasionally market research is confused with competitor research, but it is actually quite different. Market research looks at the bigger picture of what is taking place in your industry. For example if I were a soap maker I would want to know what trends are happening in the beauty industry as a whole and if I spotted the sudden trend for the use of cucumber for its anti-aging effects, then I might consider designing a range of cucumber based soaps.

Keeping on top of market research will help you to spot and understand how trends might affect your customer, so that you can offer a solution.

Regular research will show in your products and services and your customers will be watching for this. It in part helps to establish you as an expert in your field, making you the obvious company to buy from.

At the start of your journey I urge you to spend some time making your first step about research. Look at the type of products you want to make and how they sit in the market. Who would your natural competitors be, what is the market like and who is buying these products? Answering these basic questions will give you a really good start on which you can narrow your focus.

2. Narrow Your Focus

Now that you have your initial research complete you will have established who is going to buy your product, what your competition is and what the market looks like. From here we can start to narrow things down, so that we can pin 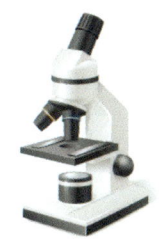 point exactly what product range we are going to start with.

I know at this point you have one hundred and one ideas in your sketch book for the things you want to make. You've probably already made a few samples! But I want you to pause for a moment, because we need to narrow these ideas down.

Launching your business successfully is going to pin itself on one thing; a focused, clear message. To achieve that we need to get super specific about what we launch first.

When I started my first craft business I had no focus and so my products were all over the place. My first box of bankrupt haberdashery stock was a real mish-mash of things from; trimmings to measuring tapes, tools to cross stitch kits. In offering such a wide range of product in small quantities I failed at several things; firstly my customers were undefinable, because they dipped in and out buying random things and secondly I was unable to keep on top of stock levels, because I had no immediate funds, or supply channels to replace them. Both things meant that I didn't have a clear idea of; who was buying, what they wanted more of and if I could even offer it. I also wasn't able to tell customers what it was I should be known for selling.

When I made changes to my business, I refocused my range and it had a wonderfully successful affect. It showed me immediately who my real customer was, what they wanted and how I needed to sell it to them.

With My Indie Life Blog I was very clear from the beginning that I was going to offer courses, eBooks and coaching to small creative businesses. My initial offer was very small and very focused, primarily on my first course 'SMASH Your Goals'[1] , which I feel is the lynch pin of having a more successful business. In being very specific and focused from the beginning I have gained traction much more quickly and become known as the 'lady who helps you be more successful in business with better planning'. From this position it is much easier for me to expand, because customers are asking me questions based on what they perceive my knowledge base to be. This information gives me fuel for new products.

---

[1] Courses found at My Indie Life Academy

How to Start a Craft Business

So ask yourself what you want to be known for. Are you the natural dyer who spins beautiful wool yarns, or are you the single parent, travel blogger who recommends the safest places to travel with your kids?

Make your focus clear and your message will be easier to give. This will inform how you set up your brand image, your website, the products you start with and the marketing you need to deliver.

3. FIND YOUR CUSTOMER

Like most, initially I got this next step the wrong way around and instead of finding my customer and building a following; I instead launched my craft products and hoped for the best.

Now whilst that might work and sales might start to come in, this method is the slow game and the more often misinformed game. You see launching first, is often based on theory, the idea that we think our customer will want our product. If we take time to find our customer first, then we can ask those questions, show them prototypes and get them interested for when we eventually launch a perfect product. This launch will be much more successful.

As designers I can see why we would naturally avoid that, given that copycats are out there. Don't miss the trick though, as we can do all of our research and interactions in a way that doesn't show every production process, or finalised design.

If we are planning to sell online, as many of us will then we need to find our customers online. Your customer research should already give you a clear idea of who that 'ideal' customer is. It may even have led you to online social groups. Start to look at what your customers are talking about and how they are interacting with each other. Start your own conversations with them and interact on their feeds. Start to become part of the community.

As a business owner this is incredibly useful to me, as it immerses me in their world. When I have new ideas, I show glimpses of them. If I have questions for my customers I ask them. I adapt my ideas and product ranges based on feedback. That's how this book came to be!

You don't need an up and running business to take this step either.

Here's an example to show you what I mean. When I was selling hand dyed yarns I would watch a lot of knitting podcasts. They became the trend for our industry. They were a really great way for me to immerse myself in my community and I even started my own podcast, which helped me sell my yarns. What I also noticed was that some of the podcasters who were knitters first and then started their own hand dyed yarn businesses were really successful straight way. Why? Because they had already found their customers and immersed themselves into their world. They talked about their plans and showed prototypes, they also asked a lot of questions. All of the feedback they got from their following helped them create a much better first product.

Your customer is everything. They are your best advocates and the food on your plate. So go and find them, love them and work with them.

4. DESIGN SOMETHING PEOPLE ACTUALLY WANT

Here's where we get back into what feels like a natural rhythm to things and we start to design.

If we have followed the first three steps, then we come to our design work with lots of useful information. We know; who our customers are, what they want from our products and we understand how to design them to be fit for purpose.

Let's work through an example here.

Say you initially want to create a range of wool yarns using natural dyes. You have started your research and you have narrowed your focus to using as many dyes as would be native to your area as possible, if you cannot grow them yourself. You also want to use British wool, because you are based in Britain. You have decided these points based on the knowledge that your customers like to know the provenance of the yarn they buy and they like to buy 'local'. With the incredible information you have learned by taking the three earlier steps, the next step of design really feels like you are able to put together a range based on what people really want.

If you had launched a range without following this process you could be suffering in slow sales, as you could have dyed wool yarn in natural dyes, but your wool provenance is not 'local', it's actually Merino from South Africa. There's nothing wrong with that yarn choice, but one tiny deviation from what your customers are really looking for can mean that you might not sell a thing!

Start your design process with intent and put your customer first. I see so many craft businesses design for their own likes and it often leads to slow sales, or their launch fails entirely. You are designing for your customer, not for you. Your customer will not buy something that they do not want.

5. Product Costings

Right about now many small businesses are itching to get their website up and list their first few items. They price their products on no more than just a little competitor research.

After a few sales, they get the creative bug that makes them want to design and make the next, even bigger batch of product. The problem is though that they soon realise that they can't make the bigger batch they'd hoped, because they don't have the funds. Why is that?

It's painfully clear at this stage that those businesses did not cost their products and services first and so have failed at the basic life support of business; *profitability*.

Before you launch anything, you need to work out all of the costings in minute detail.

When I used to sell yarn, I would wonder at the people who hadn't truly costed out their products and wonder why it was that they thought they weren't making any money, even if they had a good sales day. It came from a place of making that same mistake early on, back when I was selling on eBay. You see selling on discount platforms is all about price. You need to be the one person that sells that high value item for as little as possible and rely instead on volume trickling into a profitable cash flow. The reality for those businesses is that volume is hard to reach and hard to maintain unless you have the power of bulk ordering behind you. You need to be big, to go big, or you get swallowed up by the competition that has larger buying powers and lower expenses. It also is not a system that truly works for handmade craft businesses, which cannot decrease their labour costs enough in bulk production.

The only way to avoid the problem of failing profitability as a small business is to have a multi layered product range where the low margin items have volume sales and the higher levels of priced products make good margin on average sales. In my case that meant moving to my own website, as well as eBay so that I could have a better mix of priced product.

Before you can even imagine creating a multi-level product range you need to cost your design ideas.

How To Cost Your Idea

Costing your idea isn't difficult work, but it does need to be detailed. Here we are going to look at the basic formulae that we use to work out our figures.

How much a product costs you to make is;

> **Material cost + production costs + Labour = Cost Price**

How much can you wholesale your product for? I always recommend you create this cost, so that you can make a decision later on if wholesale is for you.

> **Cost Price x 2 = Wholesale Price**

How much will my retail customers pay?

> **Wholesale Price x 2.5 (or 3) = Retail Price**

Let's create some finer detail on those formulae shall we? You see most people don't factor in every element of financial cost when they work out their original cost price and this is where the sums don't add up later on.

How to Start a Craft Business

I'm going to use a skein of yarn as my example.

Here are the material costs;
- Yarn per 100g skein (based on a bulk buy of 1 kilo, or 10 skeins, including delivery charge)
- Dye cost (including delivery charge) based on 4 skeins dyed at once.
- Paper for ball band (based on 1 ream of card at 40gms, including delivery charge)
- Ink for printer per ball band (based on 1,000 sheet average per colour cartridge and I use 4 colours on my label, including delivery charge)
- Sellotape for the ball band (based on 1,000 skeins per reel estimate, including delivery charge)
- Plastic hang tag for shows (based on 1,000 tags per box, including delivery charge)
- Cost of any packaging required for selling (including delivery charge).

Production costs are;
- Cotton ties for dyeing the yarn
- Water cost (based on 4 skeins using 7 litres (l) per dye pot and 4l in rinsing before and 4l after)
- Electricity costs for dyeing (or gas), based on 4 skeins dyed at once.
- Electricity costs for electric spinner to get rid of excess water before drying (based on 10 skeins per load)

- Electricity costs for electric dryer (based on 20 skeins per load)

Labour costs are;
- Wage per hour based on 4 skeins taking;
    - 5 minutes to set up pre-dye rinse
    - 5 minutes to set up dye bath
    - 20 minutes to dye
    - 5 minutes to set up rinse
    - 5 minutes to spin
    - 5 minutes to load and unload dryer
    - 5 minutes to label, tag and box
    - 10 minutes to photo and list
    - 5 minutes to package for shipping

Most of the businesses I speak to forget the detail to which they need to cost at and it shows in their profitability.

Don't make the same mistake. Cost all of your design ideas and see if they are still workable in your market, i.e. will your customer pay that price? If the answer is yes, then happy days you can proceed to the next step!

If your answer is no, then you have two decisions to make. Either you choose not to proceed with that idea, because it is not financially viable, or you look at the details again. If you remove wholesale as an option will you be able to sell your product? Can you improve your production costs in order to make your cost price more viable?

If you are still stuck on how much your design idea costs, then make a sample. A sample will give you a clear indication of;
- Material cost
- Production time
- Any difficulties you need to address
- If special packaging and shipping boxes are needed
- If there are any costs you failed to see in your design work

What I'm really asking you here is, is your idea going to be profitable? You need to make profit for your business to work.

6. CREATE A BUSINESS PLAN

I can feel you questioning this next step and feeling the urge to skip the pages to step 7. After all business plans are for taking to the bank when you are seeking investment, right?

Please keep reading!

Creating a basic plan for your business is about further providing evidence for the theory of your creative business idea. It's the one thing that really helps to validate an idea and turn it into an informed business start-up.

You do not need to have the desire to create a business that ever exceeds the comforts of your spare room, but you do need to make sure that it is viable in every way and that's what a business plan provides evidence for.

A business plan needs to include;
- Customer, market and competitor research (we already started that), showing that you understand exactly who you are selling to, how and what it is that they want.
- A plan for marketing to your customer. Knowing how and where to do this successfully. You have a head start on this as you already found your

customer and have opened up lines of communication.
- A plan for how you are going to manage your business. This is the how you are going to produce, how and where you sell (and if wholesale is important), and which shows you will attend. It is also where you set out your support systems for day to day management.
- A plan for how you are going to budget and manage your accounts. We have a head start on product costings already.

What we haven't covered already will be covered in future steps, but what we are aiming for is an overall plan that we can refer to, to keep us on track to the business of our dreams.

A business plan doesn't need to be fancy if you aren't planning to ever show it to a bank, but it is really important in helping you see if your idea has real substance.

Taking your business seriously early on will help you to create a business that sustains itself and you, meaning all of those hours of hard work will be more likely to pay off.

7. CHOOSE YOUR NAME

Most of you have already toyed with the idea of naming your business at this point. You may have even started using it on your social media when you talked to potential customers about your idea.

I want you to know that at this point it is ok to make a change, but this is where you need to settle on your final name.

My advice is to pick something evocative of your brand idea.

Let's think back to the natural dyer who is creating yarns. We could call her brand 'Nature's Yarns', or 'Botanical Yarns'.

Avoid names that do not represent your brand, or product range and avoid anything that could be easily misspelt, or is derived from a slang term.

Once you have settled on a name go onto the internet and complete a domain name search. Make sure you avoid naming your business with the same name as an already established brand, as this will only cause you confusion and could hinder your future website's traffic.

Here is where I would also secure a domain name! Later on you can attach that domain name to a website, blog, or eshop.

8. DESIGN YOUR BRAND

Designing your brand is incredibly important, because it is the first thing that your customer will see and understand as an indication of what you do.

Your brand is;
- Your web design
- Your product packaging
- Your product
- Your web copy (web page writing)
- Your marketing
- Your social media
- You!

There I said it, *YOU* are your brand! Surprised?

The truth is that people buy from people. If you are a small business then you are in the unique position of being able to offer 'you' as a commodity. This is something faceless larger companies struggle with, because it is always harder to identify with something that isn't human.

Customers love that you are the person who has designed, made and sold very piece. You are the person they ask questions of and hold up as their expert in the field. Customers resonate with your message and they can join your journey. It's so much more difficult to connect with something that is an idea and not a person. It's much easier to fit a person into their social structure.

Design your brand carefully, make sure that is preaches your message in a clear and focused way. Going back to our natural dyer I would fully expect to see her branding to be whimsical, like floating botanical flowers in the breeze. Her colour choice would be clean and soft like her dyes. She would show yarns worked up in delicate shades and elegant, timeless styles. I would not expect to see bright and bold lettering or heavy newsprint text on her website. I would also not expect to see cutting edge fashion styles as samples. That would confuse me as a customer.

So make sure that at a quick glance I understand what it is you are selling, especially on your website. It is estimated that people generally give a website no more than 3-5 seconds to determine if it is worth their time. This is the same for selling in person, or delivering product to someone's home. Make sure that your presentation is branded.

9. Consider How To Sell

As crafters we have a few options for how we sell our product; online retail through our own website, or a sales platform, or we can sell in person at events, or we can choose to partly, or exclusively wholesale.

Whilst the choice is entirely down to how you want to do business, wholesale options particularly are dictated by your costings. So go back to step 5 and remind yourself of your decision on this matter. Now is the time to finalise that and amend your business plan if you need to.

Online Retail

There are a number of online options. Firstly you can create your own website using host companies, like Squarespace, EKMPowershop and Shopify. These guys provide the basic platform on which you need only add your design touch, your products and link your payment cart system. They are very reasonably priced per month and have services which you can grow into overtime.

The second option is to create your own site. You might choose something like Wordpress and any number of the plug-in services available. This needs a lot more skill and will usually end up costing you more money as you invest in web designers to do the things you can't. This doesn't make it unviable though.

The final option here is to use a selling platform like Etsy, Folksy (if you are in the UK), Amazon Handmade and so on. These are sites that are hosted and branded by the platform owners and so are limited in their service options and their customisation. They should not be ruled out however, as they have the added advantage of already having traffic looking specifically for handmade items, so you are exposed to a wider audience early on, whereas your own site will have no traffic to start with.

SHOWS

There are a number of different types of events, (all of which I talk about more in my 'Your Best Craft Show Yet' course[2]) and each has their own merits and pit falls, but essentially can open up your small business to a new revenue stream that works well alongside your online retail efforts.

I'm a big advocate for adding shows into your mix of revenue, because they can really help boost your brand's exposure. When I used to show my yarns I found that by creating a clearly branded stall I was able to secure wholesale clients, blog interviews and podcast mentions in a way that I couldn't achieve through online selling only.

---

[2] Courses found at My Indie Life Academy

WHOLESALE

Wholesale is certainly one of the options you can take if you prefer not to sell yourself or if you want to gain exposure on the high street as well as online.

Whilst the total revenue per unit is lower on wholesale orders they can work to your advantage, if the orders are regular and started at a minimum order quantity. Remember your costings here! Whilst lower margin items are ok to have as part of your product range they should be turning a higher volume of sales over time to make them profitable as a business model, especially if you are planning exclusively to wholesale.

The other thing to consider here is if you can really afford the time spent on wholesale and by this I mean that wholesale is having your products sold at half price (more or less). If you spend an enormous amount of time and energy on these products at half the price, is it worth it? Would sourcing a factory go against your business ethos?

Take the time to make this decision as it is harder to change later on, because customers rely on 'knowing' where to find you.

10. LEGALITIES

At the start of each business you will need to understand your legal obligations. For most businesses it will be as little as registering with the authorities for tax purposes, but for some other business there comes added complications of trading standards and licensing.

It is really important that you take these matters seriously, as government departments have the power to levy fines, seize assets and take penal action against those who do not comply.

HMRC REGISTRATION

Here in the UK we are required by law to announce our businesses within the tax year we open. This allows tax departments to send us the relevant paperwork during the coming tax season.

Here's a link to the UK Government website for more information;

https://www.gov.uk/government/organisations/hm-revenue-customs

If you are overseas, it is best to contact your local government to find out how business tax matters are dealt with in your country.

TRADING STANDARDS & LICENSING

Not all businesses will require further registration, or licensing, but there are certain types of businesses that do. These may include; children's toys, or some clothing businesses, food, drink and toiletry businesses, etc.

The best thing to do if you are unsure of whether your business may need special licensing is to contact your local trading standard department.

Here's a website for you;

https://www.tradingstandards.uk/consumers/support-advice

You will need to contact your local authority office.

Again if you are overseas it is best to contact your local government to find out how business license matters are dealt with in your country.

INSURANCE

Finally you will need insurance.

It is best to speak directly to an insurance broker to get the right level of insurance for your particular situation, but there are a few main areas you need to be covered for;

- Stock insurance – both on site and if you travel to shows
- Public Liability and Product Liability – these cover your service and products in regard to dealing with customers.
- General business insurance – for working from home and covering business related assets.
- Other product or service related insurances specific to your business.

It is also worth checking how your home and building insurance are affected by running your type of business from home. You may be surprised that some business practices will void these important personal insurance covers.

Taking steps to cover yourself financially and to take the correct legal footing right at the beginning of your business will ensure that you are worry free to start trading as soon as you are ready with items to sell.

11. RANGE PLAN

So far we have concentrated on creating a background to our business. We have worked out what we will sell, its financial viability and if we will consider wholesaling that product in the future, as an extra revenue stream.

Now it's time to start working on what we will deliver in terms of a complete product range and how this will work with earlier decisions, or help define them better.

Range planning is something that most small businesses will completely forget about!

WHY IS A RANGE PLAN SO IMPORTANT?

A range plan is a plan of the breadth and depth of choice in products you will be offering your customers.

It shows how many variables one product has in; colour, size, etc. this is the depth of choice. It shows how many styles of product you aim to deliver; for example how many styles of earrings, bracelets and necklaces you will have in your jewellery line.

Your range plan shows you immediately what gaps you have in your intended offer and if you need to

scale back your initial launch until you can stagger in your design ideas at a more successful later date.

This information is really key, as it helps you to establish financial budgets, effective marketing campaigns and how to adapt your business to market, consumer and economic changes that surround your business. This is how big business thinks. It does not make a pair of earrings, say 'that's nice' and then list them for sale. Everything is a strategy and it's the planning of that strategy that makes these bigger businesses generally more successful.

A very simplified range plan could look something like this on paper;

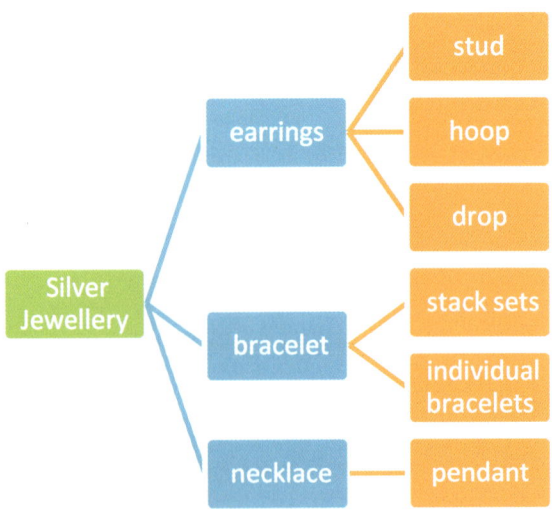

Once you have this then I suggest bringing in a cost element to your planning;

THE PYRAMID RANGE PLAN

Top £££ = high cost/price/profit, but slower sales

Middle ££ = mid cost/price/profit, but fairly regular sales

Bottom £ = low cost/price/profit, but high volume sales

Draw out financially your offer in a pyramid; drawing up from the bottom which are your easy to produce, low cost/price/profit items that are high volume and up to your high ticket items at the top.

Looking at your range plan in this way ensures that you have allowed for profit balancing, which will truly help your sales be more sustainable.

TOP LEVEL PRODUCTS

These are your high end, high ticket products. They take you the most time to make and probably cost you the most to produce. They will be a more considered sale and so won't be your highest volume pieces, or products for wholesale.

They are however really important to your range, as they are where your ultimate passion lies. They are the pieces that say the most about you as an artist.

Using our Silver jewellery example, a top level product could be a statement pendant necklace with fine, detailed silver work and semi-precious stones.

MID-LEVEL PRODUCTS

These are your 'bread and butter' pieces. They can be produced relatively easily, with reasonable costs, which mean you can sell them at a good price and make reasonable profits. You are likely to sell them every week.

These items you would probably wholesale.

Using our silver jewellery example, a mid-level product could be a slightly ornate pair of drop earrings, or a simple, but stylish bracelet.

Low Level Products

These are your less expensive items. They should not take you a long time to produce and they should be cheap to make. Your profit will come in high volume sales. This would not work as a wholesale product.

They are an important part of your brand and act as a small taster of what you specialise in.

Using our silver jewellery example, a low level product could be a simple pair of silver ball stud earrings.

As the pyramid suggests you would need to stock more of your lower end products at any one time. This is because you should be expecting high sales volume here.

Does This Work For Reproducible Items Only?

The truth is that you could use a pyramid range plan for reproducible products and unique, one-of-a-kind products. The plan itself helps you to categorise your design ideas before they become real products and in doing so dictates; budget, style content and retail price.

How to Start a Craft Business

The pyramid range plan is a useful tool regardless of your business type and it will help define and calm your creative mind, keeping finance at the top of your business agenda.

So in conclusion having a range plan in place before we create items for our website, allows us to truly think of our business, as a business and not a hobby. This is the way to a truly sustainable and long term prospect, based on profitability.

12. PRODUCTION

Making the first few items for your new business can be exhilarating. You will probably spend far longer on each piece than you need to and maybe even go over budget on your supplies. It can happen to any of us!

Here's the problem though, continuing to work in this way is a sure fire way to ruin your business financially!

Back in chapter 5 we looked at costing our original ideas. If we take this information and extend our costings to cover our new detailed range plan, then knowing what to produce and how to produce it is a little easier and certainly more financially safe.

So before you go into production, cost everything and with your accountants' hat on. You need to question the most financially beneficial ways to produce all aspects of your product. For example in my yarn business I made the decision that my low-end skeins would be made 4, or 6 at a time. Whereas the high end skeins would have luxury fibres, like cashmere and probably be made just two at a time. I also decided to buy my dyes and fixatives in bulk and switch to lower energy using burners. Little savings here and there make bigger leaps in profit.

I know all of this can sound very counter intuitive when it comes to the creative dream you had of running your own craft business, but the reality is that to stay in business you need to take care of business. Believe me setting yourself these remits early on, means that you can go wild within set boundaries when it comes to creation later on. It is how all of the bigger design businesses work and it is how they survive.

CREATING A PRODUCTION SAMPLE

There is one thing you need to do going forward at this stage and this is to create your production sample. This gives you two pieces of information; the remits for each product in materials and cost, and an idea of how long each product will take to make.

Your production sample will be a test of your budget restraints from your earlier costings and it will give you a time of manufacture per piece in your range.

Create one production sample for each range item. Make this to the standard to which you want to sell. This will allow you to use your sample for marketing and website photos.

How to Start a Craft Business

An example of the paperwork you will want to go with your sample could look like this;

- ✓ Product: Silver Ball Stud Earrings
- ✓ Cost: £3.29 per pair, based on 5 made per hour (materials + Labour)
- ✓ Exact time takes to make
- ✓ Wholesale & Retail prices
- ✓ Profit per item
- ✓ Tools:
- ✓ Notes:

Having a production sample for each product in your business files, will make them easy to refer to during the manufacture stage and easy to adapt if you need to address profitability at a later stage.

CREATING A PRODUCTION PLAN

This next stage is about scheduling.

From the sampling stage we now know exactly how long production per item takes on average. From this we can devise a plan of how long it will take us to manufacture our range to sell.

Over the page is a template that I have used in the past to create a plan of attack when it comes to producing my range. From this I can deduce; what I need to order in terms of materials, how much time I need to set aside in my weekly schedule to complete production of my range and when my range should be ready for release. Based on this I know when my website needs to be up and running by and when to start my marketing campaign.

Being logical in your approach to setting up your business will allow you to be more organised in how you deal with running it.

How to Start a Craft Business

Production Planner

Product: *Silver Stud Earrings*
Qty Needed: *5*
Deadline: *30th July 2017*

Schedule

Action	Timeframe	Being Made	Done
Prepare Silver	30 mins	Yes	Yes
Make shafts	30 mins	Yes	
Make balls	60 mins		
Total Time Needed:	2 hours		

13. PLAN YOUR MARKETING

Most of you will be thinking why am I not being advised to set up my website next? The truth is that before you can set up a website you need to know what your web copy will say (that's the text on each of your pages). You can  only be clear on this once you know what your marketing message is.

YOUR MARKETING MESSAGE

A marketing message is the language and forms in which you communicate the benefits of your brand and product. In other words it is; how you speak to your customers, how you target them and what mediums of content you show them (pictures, blogs, videos, newsletters etc.)

When you are clear on your Marketing Message you are clearer on how to put together your website, your social media, your newsletters etc. and this helps to create the right environment for your customers to find you and then buy from you.

Some businesses call their marketing message a marketing funnel.

Let's take that analogy to explain why you need to plan your marketing.

What is a Marketing Funnel?

A Marketing Funnel is the system of tracking how you target potential customers and convert them into buying customers. There are four key stages to a marketing funnel;

- Lead Generation - Creating awareness of your brand and products
- Prospect - Creating Interest in your brand and products
- Opportunity - Helping a customer's buying decision
- Client - Allowing the customer to purchase

How to Start a Craft Business

Let's look at the layers of the funnel more closely and see what aspects of your business fall into which category.

- Lead Generation – Email marketing (newsletters), social media, search engine marketing, PR (editorial, or press releases), paid adverts, events (craft shows, trade shows, etc), your website, flyers and business cards. These are all of the things that help customers to find you online and become aware of what it is that you are an expert in.
- Prospect – This is the point at which some potential customers have become interested in you enough to start following you. They are then given key incentives to peak their interest, in the forms of; targeted landing pages (or product listings), free e-books, regular email marketing (newsletters), or entry to your customer community (Facebook group, forum, etc).
- Opportunity – Some customers will have had their interest peaked at this point, especially as they feel part of your community and so strikes your 'opportunity'. Here you entice them in with things like; demos, free trials, giveaways and promotions.
- Client - At this point those who are ready to sign up and buy from you want to have uncomplicated payment systems integrated into a great customer experience.

How to Start a Craft Business

I have mentioned a lot of systems to set up at this point and so I feel it is really important to say that you don't need to do everything when you start out. It is far better that you keep it simple. That way you can create a great message from day one and layer in other beneficial systems later on.

So where do I suggest you start?

A Simple Day 1 Marketing Plan

I think at the very beginning it is really important to keep things clean, clear and simple. So consider setting up the following;

- A website with a simple to use cart system, that has been submitted to google for tracking

    https://www.google.com/webmasters/tools/submit-url

- One or two social media channels (knowing your customer and where they hang out will help you decide which platform is right for you to start on).
- An email newsletter
- A shop opening purchase offer
- Business cards

BEING CLEAR ON WHAT YOU NEED TO SAY

Earlier I mentioned the 'language' in which we need to address our customers and we didn't cover that in marketing funnels. So what do I mean by the language we need to use in our web copy?

How we talk to our customers either on our website or via social media (even video formats) is really important, because it does three things; it shows your expertise in what you do, it helps answer their questions and lastly it shows off your approachability and 'likeability'. All of these things really help solidify what your brand is synonymous with and why people should buy from you.

Your language should sell your brand in an unobtrusive manner. It should speak to your customers on their terms. So when creating your copy, remember to;
- Answer your customers most frequently asked questions about your product or service
- Show them how your product or service solves their problem
- How buying into your product and service helps them now

By defining how you want to speak to your customers and in what forms early on, allows you to set up these systems much more easily.

14. SET UP YOUR WEBSITE (OR SALES PLATFORM)

At this point in our fledgling business we are clear about what we will be selling and how we will be selling it. What we need to decide on next is where to sell it.

As product makers there are a couple of options; to sell via our own website, or to use a sales platform like Etsy, Amazon, eBay, etc. I'm not going to dictate which of these options I think is best; instead I want you to be clear about your decision before we continue. If you were to ask my opinion on which to choose though, I'd be honest and say both have their merits and I personally chose a combination of both options, as have many, many others. Take a look at what's on offer and which you think would best suit your brand and products.

I do want to talk about what you need to set up on your site, because this is really important and often neglected.

WHAT EVERY WEBSITE NEEDS

First and foremost your website needs to adhere to the look and message of your brand and marketing, so make sure that you think about design, layout and your choice of wording.

When you are ready with this then make sure you have;
- A good 'Home' page – This should be clear on what it is you sell. Keep it clean, simple and inviting.
- An 'About' page – This should tell everyone who visits your site who you are and why you are selling what you sell.
- A form of contact – Customers should have a way to contact you easily.
- Easy to navigate product listings – You need to show your product catalogue clearly and make the cart system easy to use.
- An easy to read 'Terms and Conditions' Page – If you are selling anything online you need to make sure that you are clear about how your customers are entering into a sales contract with you and what that means for them. Make sure to include what happens if something goes wrong, as this is your opportunity to alleviate any confusion about how you handle your business. I always include a copyright clause here too, so that people know that they cannot copy my work. You may wish to extend this to include a policy on other websites using your images or content too, or if you allow customers to

resell your work. See chapter 18 if you need more advice on this).
- A simple cookie and privacy policy – This tells your customers how using your site affects them. The use of cookies as data collection points is standard practice on websites these days, so having a simple policy in place helps customers to understand what data you are collecting from their visit and how, or if this is stored. There are free policy generator tools on the web for you, so search Google.

I also want to make a quick point about wholesale before we move on. Generally as this is a different part of your business to the retail front end of your website, I suggest that you draw up wholesale terms as a separate document that you send with wholesale contracts. Publishing these online is not advisable, unless you only choose to wholesale your products or services.

Sit down and plan your website before you start. This will allow you to create the perfect platform for your customers to buy into you and what you sell.

It will also help graphic and web designers understand what you need.

15. BEAUTIFUL PHOTOS

I see a lot of creatives struggle when it comes to photos, because let's face it we weren't all born to wield a camera to David Bailey's professional standards, try as we might! There are however, some key points we need to convey in our pictures;

- What our product looks like
- What our product is for, or how it works
- Our brand message

More than that our website and product listings act as a portfolio of our work and as such they should 'wow' our customers. You need to consider lighting, location and the style of your shot.

The images should always be at a high resolution, in other words very clear and crisp. You can achieve great photography with a smart phone these days so don't be fooled into thinking you need to start out with an expensive camera. If you do want to invest then DSLR cameras (Digital Single-Lens Reflex cameras) are often used.

THE DIFFERENCE BETWEEN WEB IMAGES AND PRODUCT LISTING PHOTOGRAPHS

There are two different types of images you will take with your products; firstly general web images that you can use both on your site and for marketing and then secondly the product listing photo. There are vast differences between what these should look like and why.

THE WEB PRODUCT IMAGE

When planning these images I often ask myself the question 'How would Vogue shoot this?', because these images are the 'fashion photo shoot' for your product. They tell your customer how your product can be used, how great it feels to be using it and excites the customer into finding out more. In other words these are the pretty magazine images that will lead the customer into your shop.

How to Start a Craft Business

Photo Credit Sara's Texture Crafts

Here's an example from my own past product business Sara's Texture Crafts, where I sold hand dyed yarns. In the example you can see one of my yarns in use. So I am being clear that you can knit with my yarns and this is how the dye technique comes out. I might also create an image where I show the yarn being worn. This will tell my customers how great my yarn is to wear.

How to Start a Craft Business

Photo Credit Sara's Texture Crafts

THE PRODUCT LISTING PHOTOGRAPH

Your product photos are much more basic in comparison, because they do not have any magazine style to them, instead they are functional pictures. They tell your customer exactly what the product looks like, so they know what to expect when it arrives.

In my example (over page) I am showing my customers how my hand dyed yarns, although from the same batch can appear different to the eye. This is important if your product will vary slightly from item to item of the same design.

How to Start a Craft Business

Photo Credit Sara's Texture Crafts

The other thing to remember is that this image shows much more clearly the indication of colour, shape and size too, if that's important.

There might be several product photos in your listings and this will depend on how complex your product is. So think about your product and ask yourself 'what does my customer need to know?' If I were selling bags, then I would need to show what the lining looks like inside, if there is a difference between the front and back of the bag, if there are inside pockets, how the bag closes and so on. Each product image should reflect one of these aspects and show it clearly.

Think about your photographs and plan how you need to take them ahead of time. This will help you maximise your product, website and marketing with the right photos in the right places.

16. MAILING LIST

Setting up your mailing list early on is the *right* way to start your business. I think people feel somehow that they have to have lots to say or sell before they can start fostering their community and that simply isn't true.

In 2017 it is widely understood that email marketing is still the most effective way to direct sell your products online, outstripping social media campaigns for regular income conversions. So it's more important than ever to create a newsletter list for your website as you launch, even if you do nothing more than send out an automated welcome message with a coupon code initially.

To set up your mailing list, you first need to find a host. There are many options out there and some cost more than others. Personally I have used www.mailchimp.com for years (for free) and I have always found them to be easy to use for simple start-up businesses. I have also been recommended hosts such as www.convertkit.com and www.activecampaign.com. Take a look and see which offers you the package you would make most use of.

How to Start a Craft Business

Get your list setting complete and then insert a 'widget' onto your website in a prominent home page position. Mine looks like this on My Indie Life Blog;

This will drip feed anyone interested in your products to sign up to become part of your community. You can then take some time to plan what it is you want to say in each newsletter and how frequently you wish to send them.

If you sell via an online sales platform like; Etsy, Amazon and eBay then it is less likely that you will have an email marketing option (although I do know that eBay once had a very basic newsletter option incorporated in their premium shop package). This is because you don't 'own' your customers or transactions, the host does. The hosts will wish to control the way in which their customers frequent and interact with their platform and marketing. In these cases a mailing list is harder to implement, but is still possible. So think about starting a blog and using that as a base for your website. Or, you could have a standalone ecommerce website as well as a sales platform shop. Consider your options and choose which suits you and your business, and then point your platform customers here.

The key things to remember when sending your newsletters is that they should adhere to your marketing message, so they should be branded, they should talk to your customer in the way you want your message to be conveyed and above all they should include your customer in your journey. Remember that your customer has chosen to allow you to contact them, so engage and get to know them. As well as making sales, your newsletter is a great way to research your customer base!

17. Plan Your Social Media

We talked initially, back in chapter 13 about the importance of starting out simple and I stand by that when it comes to your social media choices.

You know two things at this point in your start-up; firstly where your customer is hanging out and secondly how you wish to convey your message to them.

Pick just two social media channels from your research, ideally the channels that your customer thrives on. Then you need to create your first marketing campaign.

What Is A Marketing Campaign?

A Marketing Campaign is a series of content that you create to direct your potential customer to firstly become aware of you and secondly do one thing (a 'Call to Action' as they call it in marketing).

Traditionally a marketing campaign would have included; printed media, radio and television, particularly for larger businesses and while print media is still an option for smaller start-ups it is ever more likely that social media is the first choice you will take.

How to Start a Craft Business

As you are readying the launch of your website, then your first campaign is to tell your customers about who you are and where they can find you (your website). You are going to do this over a series of social posts, because content posted to social networks isn't seen by everyone and doesn't have a long life span, so you need to create lots of different content to create a wider awareness.

Your content can be;
- A photo with wording
- A computer generated graphic with/without text
- A line, or paragraph of text
- A video
- A viral GIF (an image that animates a series of moving or static images into quick frame)
- A photo montage, or slide show
- An early testimonial

Each piece of content should be clear on what you sell, who you are and where they can find you online.

Next you need to decide how regularly and for how many days you need to post your content. Most businesses tend to cover more important campaigns over 30 days, posting at least twice a day on the subject. Think about how that could work for you and schedule that in - It's quite ok to post just once a day, or every other day if that works better for you.

CAN I AUTOMATE MY SOCIAL MEDIA?

Absolutely, in fact I encourage it!

Unfortunately it doesn't cut the time you spend creating your content, but it does mean that once you have all of your content created you can preschedule it using online tools. This will leave you plenty of time for other things like; customer queries, production and delivering your products.

I use both; www.hootsuite.com and www.buffer.com and both have free versions of their services. Again there are lots of other service providers out there, so have a look.

DON'T FORGET ENGAGEMENT

It is really important that you don't just post your social content and run, because the key part of social media is that it is 'social'! So spend some time each day interacting with your community and making connections. This will help grow your brand awareness and help to increase the likelihood that people will want to listen to your carefully crafted message.

18. Friendly & Professional Customer Service

Behind every great business empire is a great customer service plan and so it's really important to make sure you have your first plan in place before you open your website up to trade.

A good customer service plan has a very clear set of terms and conditions for how your customers interact with your business. This tells them how you do what you do, how the process of buying from you will work and what legal, or contractual obligations you hold a transaction bound to. It also gives clear indication of what to expect from you if they have an issue at any stage of your interaction, or transaction.

Typically for a small product based business, terms would include;
- when and how payment should be made
- who owns the products or services before any payment is made
- who is responsible for the goods or services during a transaction
- details of how items will arrive with the customer
- details of third party policies, i.e. shipping, ownership and responsibility.
- any health and safety warnings

- details of a return or exchange policy, including the timeframe and condition in which these are accepted
- copyright agreement
- details on resale

Take a look at how bigger businesses set these up on their site to get an idea of how you might phrase things. If you have access to someone from a legal background (retail law) then this would help enormously. If not then contact your local authority's trading standards division. I have always found them very helpful on legalities.

A great customer service plan extends on from these basics.

PRESENTATION

Presentation is the act of how you conduct yourself in dealing with your customer. So it's how you phrase your emails, or answer the phone. It is also how you conduct your brand message.

Think about what you expect from companies you do business with and how you expect them to deal with you. Your customers will expect the same from your business.

REPUTATION

Your business can be both made and broken by what your customers think of you, so it's really important that you try to manage your business reputation as best as possible in an authentic way. This does not mean deleting the odd bad comment here or there, or paying for people to give you good reviews, instead it means showing your customers that you care.

Dialogue is really key here, so as your social media channel fills up with dedicated followers, or your newsletter becomes more engaged don't forget to ask for customers' input and reviews. This is a great way to see what your customers really think and if something needs changing.

Seeing you grow over time and how you handle yourself in a professional and caring way will only spawn more and more loyalty.

DEALING WITH PROBLEMS

There's no way to avoid the odd problem, whether it be a miscommunication, a return, or something else. All businesses will face this. It's a fact of business. Please don't take this personally; I know that is harder said than done.

In the early years of my yarn business I sold primarily on eBay, although I had a small, growing website and an Etsy shop. eBay was hard! Sometimes it felt like an uphill battle between me and what seemed like endless scams, but it was an important part of my business as its turn over capacity was by far my biggest. So I laboured on.

Very occasionally I'd have the odd email asking for an exchange, or a return and even rarer I'd have things go missing in the post. At that time I was a 'Gold Seller', which meant I had a special status on eBay with a dedicated Business Support Manager. I'd find myself talking to him more and more as time went on about how to maximise sales and how to deal with things that weren't going quite right. I remember he once asked me to put my 'big girl pants on' one day after I'd taken an unprovoked and very heated email from a customer rather badly. I was incredibly affronted at first when I put the phone down, 'how dare he!' It seemed very patronising and very sexist.

But in the basics of his message he was right.

And he was right to be blunt with me (although I still wish he'd chosen a different phrase to catch my attention).

The cold business truth is that you have to take out that deep emotion and connection with what you do at those moments when things are going wrong, step back and make the right decision for your customer and your business.

The right thing to do is to settle the dispute in favour of the customer, pick yourself up, learn from it, adapt from it and move on.

As simple as that.

Remember presentation and reputation at all times.

So thank you Stefan where ever you are, that lesson learned was a lesson that has stuck with me.

Great customer service is a work in progress. It is not something that will be 'great' overnight, especially as you start out in a new business. So my advice is to spend some time thinking about how you want to deal with situations as they arise, what you want to be known for and how you can make your brand of customer service happen.

19. ACCOUNTS & BUDGETS

If you are the type of business owner who wants to keep receipts in a shoe box and worry about money when it comes to filing your tax return, then look away for a moment.

Bangs head against desk

Ok, are you back?!

Let's start with why that's no longer good enough!

Building a sustainable and profitable business comes from knowing your figures inside and out, from what you have coming in, to what you have going out and also what you budget for certain parts of your business.

SPREADSHEETS ARE YOUR FRIEND

A simple spreadsheet, set up well, will calculate essential information from; your cash flow profit, to what areas of sales you are excelling at and what areas of the business you are over spending on, etc. So go and take a course if you have to, but learn how to use a spreadsheet for your accounts.

If you prefer not to rely on a spreadsheet, then open an account with an accounting software provider.

BUDGETING

Take the opportunity to put budgets on spending and stick to it. Especially when you are starting out there are lots of things you feel you'd like to buy, or subscribe to. Question everything, do you really need it?

Remember when you start getting regular sales you can rethink what you invest in and what you buy.

REVIEW YOUR ACCOUNTS REGULARLY

Setting up a spreadsheet and a budget on it's own is not enough, in fact if left it's almost as bad as the shoe box scenario! So make sure to schedule in time each week and then each quarter to update your figures and to review them. Look at what your figures are telling you, do you need to take action?

Staying on top of your money from the beginning is really crucial. You can only stay in business for as long as it is profitable to do so and so understanding and knowing what your numbers are can really help you make decisions that will sustain your business in the long run.

20. SCHEDULE YOUR TIME

You only have one pair of hands. Those hands need to make everything you sell, create the marketing to help sell those products and to then deliver them to your customer. So how do you get it all done and have enough time to lead the path of your business?

You need a schedule.

Buy yourself a planner, or create a spreadsheet for each month. You could even sign up to online scheduling tools if that helps. This can be as simple or as complicated as you like, but make sure it's something that works for you.

Then sit down and plan.

The important thing about scheduling is that it needs to work for you and be flexible enough to add things in, or to adapt to how your business changes going forward. So just like your accounts and budgets keep your schedule under constant review.

21. SUPPORT SYSTEMS

There are two types of support system you need to consider for your business;

STREAMLINING SYSTEMS

Streamlining systems are the little systems you put into place early on that help you to streamline your actions and time in certain areas of your business. They also help give you focus. An accounting system is a great example, because it allows you to know your figures inside and out. It also saves you time in the action of finding out key information when required, like how much you spend on printer ink, for example.

Systems like this can be either things that you set up, or things that you buy into. So going back to the accounting example you could create your own spreadsheet, or invest in an online software application.

Think about what you could streamline from day one to save you time as you grow. What can you set up today?

Immediately I can see a need for;
- An accounts system
- A time schedule
- A production plan
- A range plan

- Costing sheets
- A research journal
- Marketing funnel and message plan
- Social Media plan and scheduler
- Customer service plan

You could also look at systems for specific parts of your business, like production. When I dyed yarn, having 'x' amount of ring burners could increase my batch yield, over just one burner. As my business grew that could have extended to a stand-alone oven system increasing it further. It would have saved me time, action and cost.

SOUND BOARD SUPPORT

This is the intangible support that goes a long way to helping you cope mentally and emotionally with running a small business. It's a friend, or a family member, it is a group of fellow entrepreneurs that you have something in common with.

The most important thing about this group is that they are a sounding board for your ideas, questions and fears. You shouldn't feel afraid to ask them anything, even if it feels like you are missing an obvious answer.

I run a [group on Facebook](#) just for this purpose.

22. SET GOALS

In order to grow your fledgling business to a sustainable full time proposition you need to create targets for growth. I created a fully streamlined framework for my business which I teach in my 'SMASH Your Goals' course[1] and in my product business it is what helped me grow from my £100 investment to almost 7 figures of turnover, more importantly making a profit while I was doing it.

It's a massive subject and one I'm not sure I can capture in just a few pages... but let me try.

Think of your business as a building.

Planning underpins everything that you do well in your business, like a building's foundation and it particularly works well if it is informed planning. What do I mean by that? Being informed about how your business is working and where you want it to get to is one thing, but the detail of knowing how to get to this imagined future business is the position of knowing exactly the right target to set yourself at the right time.

---

[1] Courses found at My Indie Life Academy

How to Start a Craft Business

It's like building a house with an architectural drawing. You know exactly what layer of what type of bricks to put down next.

In my [Facebook group](#) I run quarterly challenges that I call '30 Days of Action'. The idea is that we take one concept from our imagined wish list of things we'd like for our business and make them happen, such as creating a mailing list, or increasing our newsletter subscribers. The challenge sees me teach you how to create a goal, plan tasks from it and then tackle it day by day until it's done on day 30. Come join us!

Most people think that this act alone can be repeated to fulfil the goal setting obligations they have in their business.

The truth is that it is not enough on its own. In fact that's building your business house without an architectural plan. You are just putting bricks down where you feel like. Now they might be great individual bricks and go together to make some fine brickwork, but there's no logic to your planning and no logic to your growth and so the finished business house might not look how you expected it to.

Good business is not made better by plucking an idea out of thin air and making it work for your business because you have a whim for it that day. Good business is built on careful planning of where each brick of your business building goes and what the building should look like at the finish.

Consider how you set goals for your business and set them to push yourself forward in a logical way.

23. KEEP MOTIVATED

Owning your own business and running it successfully is hard work. Really hard work. It will take long hours and above all focus and determination. So it's really important to keep your motivation levels up.

There are a couple of tricks I'm going to share with you about how to feel more motivated and inspired to work on your business, but before we get there let's talk about spotting a lack of motivation.

HOW TO SPOT YOUR LACK OF MOTIVATION

There are a few signs that show you are feeling less motivated about something and they can be easy to spot. They all point to your best efforts at avoidance;

- You are acting restless and easily distracted.
- You start tasks not on your to do list.
- You get a little sharp tongued if pushed about a certain topic, or task.
- You suffer a creative block and can't seem to start a task.
- You feel a bit overwhelmed, or confused.

These are all perfectly normal feelings and you aren't alone in feeling them, but they are negative feelings and this is where you need a change.

WWW.MYINDIELIFEBLOG.NET

You need just a spark of inspiration to get that positive feeling of motivation back.

Explore What Makes You Feel Unmotivated

Understanding why you are feeling particularly unmotivated stems from a deeper understanding of what it is that is upsetting you the most.

Look at what you had to do today – can you spot a task, or a situation that you didn't really want to do? Something that might have been holding you back from completing a task… How did you feel about that?

Why You Feel Unmotivated

There are a couple of things that are making you feel a lack of motivation for that task or situation you are avoiding.

Fear. You feel you are incapable or uncomfortable about your task today. Something is making you feel unable to perform at your best and when we feel like this it is natural to try and avoid it.

You didn't set yourself this goal, or you didn't have a clear goal today. Sometimes we feel a better sense of productivity when we are working towards goals we set ourselves. This is because we get a sense of pleasure and pride from achieving a target we set for ourselves. Make sure you are setting goals that work for you and your business, not someone else's idea of what's best.

You aren't clear on why you need to do what you are tasked to do today. Occasionally we don't fully understand why we are supposed to be doing something, even though we are told it will be good for us, and so we get a little mentally stuck, or feel a bit petulant about it.

All of these pain points leave you with a negative mind-set and this is what is really stopping you.

You need to change that feeling into something more positive. From that point you should feel naturally more inclined to have a go at what you have been avoiding.

10 THINGS TO DO TO FEEL MORE MOTIVATED

1. **Set better goals** – if you have a set of clear, actionable goals then you will feel naturally more inclined to work on them, because you understand what you need to be doing and when. More than that, breaking down your goals into manageable tasks gives you an easier checklist to tick off. The feeling of being successful at something is a very positive thing.
2. **Understand your 'why'** – sit down and think about the bigger picture of why you need to be doing something. When you are clear on your 'why', you will feel happier to work towards it.
3. **Do a bit of research** – sometimes you will get stuck because you just can't figure out the best way to approach a task. That can be an easy fix if you spend a little time doing some research and

once that light bulb comes on in your head, you will find it easy to get to work.
4. **Ask for help** – if you are really feeling unconfident about doing something then ask for a little help. There is no shame in that and everyone needs it. If you have a friend or family member who can walk with you to that big meeting, or go through your task breakdown with you over coffee, then do that. If you have an on-line connection who is great at helping keep you accountable for projects, then ask them to help you through your block. You will find that they can be incredibly useful at showing you in the nicest way that you CAN do this.
5. **The 10 minute tidy up** – this sounds like such a little thing, but believe me it really helps. Just start with your work desk and do a bit of filing. In no time at all you will be feeling on top of things again.
6. **Take a break and recharge** – however you choose to take a break, make sure it is a break from everything. Switch off your phone, go for a walk, sit in the park, do some laps of the local pool. Whatever it is, it needs to be a clear break from your working environment and a break from the things you find most distracting. You will come back to your tasks with a sense of refreshment and that positive feeling will show in your productivity.
7. **Get a 10 minute fix of HAPPY** – What could you do right now for 10 minutes that will make you feel happier? Could you put on some head phones and listen to your favourite upbeat record? Could you make yourself a cup of coffee and sit for a bit? Whatever your 'happy' is go and do it... mine is dancing around the living room to a good dance

track, like no-one can see me... Arms everywhere and singing at the top of my voice!

8. **Knowing when you are feeling naturally motivated** – Sometimes it's all about timing. If you are more of a morning person, then move all of the more difficult tasks to the beginning of the day. If you are someone who likes the sense of productivity then pepper your bigger, heavier tasks with small, quick-step tasks. By utilising your time in a way that works of you, you will naturally feel more motivation to get things done.

9. **Rewards** – This seems like a frivolous thing, or maybe even something slightly childish to do for yourself, but it really isn't. The fact is that people respond to incentives. Now I'm not suggesting that you go shopping after you tick something off of your to do list... oh my I'd be in trouble with my credit card if I did that! What I am saying is that sometimes we should reward a job well done. Rewards can be simple and cost no money at all. They can be working hard all week on a big task so that you can finish work early on a Friday. They can be treating yourself to a slice of cake from the deli if you get through some of your least favourite parts of the job. I eat a slice of cake while I'm filing... I'm not going to lie... it's become an institution in my business!

10. **Walk away** – If all else fails then ask yourself if you really want to do what you have tasked yourself to do. For example, if you feel like you should be hosting a podcast on YouTube because you realise that it might be a great time to get into video marketing for your business, but you just can't sit down and get your act together for

filming... then maybe YouTube videos aren't for you? Maybe what you are asking of yourself is an unnatural task for you. Maybe you need to think of another way to market your business that is much more natural to you. Or maybe you should send your products off to the best YouTubers for review, instead of putting yourself in front of the camera? There could be a way around your block that helps you achieve a desired goal in a much healthier and positive way. So while I'm saying walk away, I guess what I really mean is re-evaluate and look for an alternative.

Motivation is the guiding force behind our attitude to our work and can be something that occasionally we struggle with. So do you best to keep on top of it! If you need help then join other small business owners in my Facebook group.

24. SET UP YOUR WORKSPACE

Often as creative people we can seem a little disorganised. The spaces we use to create our art can, to us, feel like an organized chaos, but to others seem like a nightmare of hoarding meets mad science! That works for us,  as we potter around drawing new ideas down on napkins and building wildly unique creations, but it does not work for business. Good business unfortunately does require us to have a sense of structure.

When you first start out you will need the following to make your business days more productive in time, output and creation;

- Computer (desktop or laptop), printer and internet connection.
- Desk and chair – a space to have your computer, to also work on new designs and shipping
- Small filing cabinet – to hold your accounts and any important paperwork
- Photography set up – somewhere that has good light to stage your product photos.

My advice is to set yourself 'working hours' and let everyone around you know what those are, so that you are not disturbed while you work with non-business related issues. Then let your customers know so that your 'out of hours' are your own.

The key to this set up is that you opt for tools that suit your business and allow you to be productive in output and creativity. It should also be a space that promotes focus.

25. WORK ON IT EVERY DAY

I often see small creative businesses making the mistake that their hobby turned into a business is still in fact a hobby. They play at doing a little bit of production here and there, coupled with a few sporadic photos posted to social media.

Nothing is consistent.

The upshot of this is that their business turnover is inconsistent and they wonder why.

The other thing I sometimes hear is that partners aren't taking their business seriously either and asking questions like; 'when are you going to get a proper job?'

The problem is that they can't see consistent earnings, or success either, because you are being inconsistent.

My answer is always the same.

Imagine your business is a machine that produces money. There are lots of parts to that machine; production, design, marketing, sales, customer service, accounting and so on. A machine needs a battery to work effectively. Without a full battery the machine will start to lose power and slow output until it grinds to a halt, therefore ceasing to produce money. A stopped cold machine is always harder to re-start!

So to maintain a business you need to work on it consistently and have all parts of it working in harmony to produce your turnover.

Regardless of whether you have eight hours, or one hour to work on your business each day, book out that time to work on your goals and your daily to do list. Working consistently over time will bring you greater results.

Results are also the best way to bring around those 'nay-sayers'!

26. CONFIDENCE IS PRACTICE

I must confess that this is one of the chapters that took me the longest time to sit down and write. You see just like you I struggle with confidence from time to time and so I wasn't sure I'd be the best person to advise you.

Then it hit me.

Confidence is something that is learned.

We start our businesses knowing little about who our customers really are, what the market is like and how to run a successful business. We worry every day that we don't know what we are doing, or that we don't know how to make this little machine work. We start our research and little by little we start to learn how to answer those earlier questions. We gain confidence and those foundation business practices become second nature.

We move onward.

We hit a new confidence brick wall. Maybe it's around better targeting our clients within marketing, or which product lines we should expand. Maybe it's about sales growth, or taking our business full time.

How to Start a Craft Business

We feel like we are back at square one; unconfident, unhappy and anxious.

What bigger businesses do at this point is to remove the confidence element and sit down to plan how they are going to overcome this obstacle. They might move on to educate themselves in how to solve their own problem, or they might seek help by hiring a consultancy, or an outside service.

As small businesses financially it's not always possible to hand the work to someone more qualified. So here is our opportunity to grow by learning. Go back to chapter 22 for a moment and refresh yourself on the idea of goal planning. This is a tool I use to set myself learning, or obstacle based experiments. I take what's troubling me at that moment and plan a goal and tasks around solving that problem. I spend time chipping away at that knowledge gap. By the end of the goal I hope to answer my earlier concern and put something into place that benefits the growth of my business.

Once the problem is solved I can move on knowing that I now know how to answer my problem and I have learned a new confidence.

I look back at the successful craft business I had for 11 years and I know first-hand the painful feeling that a lack of confidence dealt me, but I can also see an amazing amount of growth. Growth I created for myself in not only the handling of my business but also my confidences, as those new practices became a seamless part of my day to day.

So when you feel unconfident do two things; understand what it is you are unconfident about and do something about it, then secondly look back at just how far you have come already. Count your successes and celebrate them. You did that, you did all of it!

Every business owner will tell you that running your own business, even a vastly successful one is like riding a rollercoaster, both emotionally and figuratively. It's how you learn to pick yourself up and out of those downward moments that make you tough and I believe it's because you have learned new confidences.

To this end I firmly believe today that while I don't think any one business owner has it all figured out, their confidences have been learned and grow in number every day… and yours will too.

27. KEEP RESEARCHING

In chapter 1 we talked extensively about research and the need to concentrate that research in some key areas; customer, market, competitor. We also took time to understand that this process of research is ongoing.
Here I want to highlight that list again and also add to it.

Going forward once we have set up and launched our business we need to continually look for information about;

Our customers changing habits – Over time customers will change their minds and habits regularly. In order to be able to respond to that we need to be aware of what those changes look like and how they affect our current business in terms of products and service.

We should also consider our own experiences with customers. Have we come across areas that they have highlighted in feedback that indicate a trend?

What are our competitors doing – Competitors change regularly too. At the beginning of the year you will find lots of new businesses in your niche popping up as people embark on their own independent journey. Be mindful of these seedling businesses, as they can really change up customer's view of what your niche industry looks like. Also be mindful of existing competitors, check to see how they are growing and changing over time. Have they spotted opportunities, or changes you need to be aware of?

What is the market place telling us? – The economic plain is ever changing and so this is something to look out for, as it will predict levels of disposable income for your type of product. It will also influence competition levels too. There may be trends in pricing too that are affected by economic climates, so look out for that.

Look at the craft market as a whole, not just your niche. What is happening out there? You will find that trends develop in different niche hobbies. This may indicate a knock on effect to your trading capability. Knowing this in advance can help you react to the betterment of your business.

Watch your Stats – Statistics give us hard data to interpret. Keeping on top of them and monitoring them means we notice 'blips' we can move on quickly. So monitor your social statistics, your email campaigns, your account figures and see if these are telling you things you may need to act on.

How to develop our skills – Quite often the information that we gather in our research will take us down the path of action that may be in an area we are unfamiliar with and so there is a need to develop our skills to solve the problem. Be open to this and embrace it.

The more up to date you are with research, the more informed your choices are and you start to create more opportunities for your business.

28. REMEMBER TO BE THE BOSS

I watch a lot of people struggle with keeping their heads above water, with knowing what step to take next and how to gain more success for their business.

They are always so very busy though.

They are hidden in mounds of paperwork at the weekends and endlessly finishing production for a website update just hours before they are due to go live, even staying awake half the night just to finish on time.

So when I ask them what their goal plan looks like, or how they are automating their accounts they look at me blankly for a second, before defiantly announcing that they just simply don't have time to do that!

On the occasions where I get an answer I can see that the proposed solutions are just band aids. They aren't fully thought out.

So why am I getting these answers from clients?

The answer is that it's all about their mind-set and how their mind-set governs their approach to their business.

THE EMPLOYEE MIND-SET

For most of us, the reality is that we came from jobs where we were employed by someone else.

That someone else did all of the planning and 'bigger picture' thinking to drive the business forward. They created forward action by delegating tasks to their employees on a daily, or weekly basis in a logical way. They also hired and fired staff.

We were not required to think bigger than the tasks set (although initiative was most probably welcomed). So quite naturally we did only what was asked of us; to concentrate on the daily tasks.

We accepted the employee mind-set.

Adopting this mind-set is perfectly natural when working for someone else, but not transferable when we start our own business. Yet for some reason we continue in this fashion, I guess out of familiarity.

Things soon start to feel out of control in our business when the business starts to dictate what things we need to do and when. The problem is that our business cannot tell us how to plan, how to automate and how to implement the right systems to have us 'the employee' working effectively.

So our business success demands we start with a very different mind-set. The mind-set of the Boss and those who have found success in what they do, will have consciously slipped into this new pattern of thinking early on.

THE BOSS MIND-SET

To be the boss of your new business you need to start thinking like you *own* the business. It really isn't any harder than that.

You need to;
- Look at the bigger picture on a regular basis
- Plan goals to move the business forward
- Schedule projects and tasks in a logical way
- Plan finances
- Plan marketing
- Plan production
- Review and adapt plans, projects and tasks
- Hire new staff if needed

I could go on... but do you see a pattern?

At every stage I have mentioned, or inferred to planning.

The boss of the business doesn't get their hands dirty on every task, instead they manage it. Part of managing well is planning well.

WHY PLANNING WORKS.

Planning gives you an element of control, quite simply.

By having a controlling hand on your business you are more likely to spot mistakes before they happen, foresee times when workloads will be harder and create the right actions or systems for success at the right time.

Planning does take time, but trust me when I tell you that it is time well spent and that it is long-term time saved.

So start thinking like the Boss of your business and plan!

It's not to say that you won't ever need to wear your employee's hat again, particularly if you have no employees.

You will always need to wear that old hat. It is the hat that gets everything done on the day-to-day.

But what really helps you get things done in a way that is not overwhelming and dare I say it

motivational, is knowing that you came to this task from a Boss' perspective and so you know that you are doing the right task, on the right day to move your business forward in the right way.

29. KEEP REVIEWING

All businesses need review from time to time, even small craft businesses. Review is a healthy approach to understanding where your business is compared to where you want it to be.

My advice is to set up regular intervals at which you sit down; pen, paper, your accounts and your statistics and review every part of your business. Look at things like;

- what stock you are holding
- your product range
- your production methods
- your costings
- your sales and expenditure
- your marketing and conversions

Combine this with your customer, competitor and market research and evaluate everything and then re-evaluate your future plans.

Taking this approach means that you are much more clued into what your business looks like today and what it is asking for next. This then allows you to make decisions based on what you need to do to align that with your core desire for your business.

30. NEVER BE AFRAID TO EVOLVE

In the 11 years I worked at my product based business it evolved tremendously. Sometimes that evolution was a natural growth and in a couple of cases it was forced by my own hand.

Evolution will happen naturally and is led by customer and market changes. Trends cause the need for evolution. This is not a bad, or a scary thing. In fact a good business will spot these coming and adapt in a way that your customers will almost miss happening entirely. This is the healthy approach you should be taking to your business.

Sometimes you need to force changes though. These cases are much rarer and are usually based around profitability, sales, or the need to change operationally. Sometimes it's also about realigning your business with your core values and your business mission. Again these are healthy reactions to a well organised business, but they are much more noticeable to your customer.

Each forced evolution in my business was planned, reviewed, and agonized over. Sometimes I'd feel so self-conscious in making the forced choices, that I would put them off until the very last moment. I guess I was worried about judgement and unconfident in my decisions. The

truth was that in those cases the changes I made led to making my business better (operationally and financially).
So don't be afraid change. Change is natural and change can be good… scary sometimes, but essentially a good thing.

The most important thing to keep in mind is that you need to be happy in your business and your business needs to be able to provide. So if you need to change something then change it!

CONCLUSION

Running your own business takes time and an amount of grit. There is no 'one size fits all' solution to being successful quickly, but with passion and focus the work feels easier.

Having a craft business in particular is no different; it is a business that needs nurturing and fuelling to succeed.

In this short eBook I hope to have given you a good starting point to realising your own independent journey and a lot of the principles that other business owners simply won't tell you about. I hope to have inspired you to take your very first steps from a much more organised and informed place.

I know you can do this.

I know, because I did it and the truth is I'm no-one special, I'm an artist and a crafter just like you. I have no special business qualifications, just a bountiful leap in experience at this point, which is all something you will learn along the way. I promise!

So go. Go start your journey and enjoy it.

Sara x

ABOUT THE AUTHOR

I come from a creative product background where I turned my initial £100 investment into a six figure business in a niche area of the craft industry.

Throughout this time I taught a lot of colleagues and customers different aspects of what I did, so it seemed only natural to package these tools up and put them out there into the world.

In 2017 My Indie Life Blog was born - a place where fellow independent makers can find the essential tools they need to push their business forward and create the jump-out-of-bed job they always wanted!

**I Want To Help You Feel
Motivated + Confident + Successful**

Find out more at [My Indie Life Blog](#).

How to Start a Craft Business

Other Books By Sara Millis

eBooks by www.myindielifeblog.net

In this 30 day challenge I aim to help you improve your Etsy shop look, layout and productivity for better sales and customer service.

EBook is available on Amazon.

ISBN-10: 153999726X
ISBN-13: 978-1539997269

FREE VIDEO WORKSHOPS BY MY INDIE LIFE BLOG

I host a number of free workshops to evolve your business learning. You can find them over on my Academy.

Printed in Great Britain
by Amazon